BUSINESS PORTRAITS

APPLE

Published by VGM Career Horizons,
a division of NTC Publishing Group
4255 West Touhy Avenue
Lincolnwood (Chicago),
Illinois 60646-1975,
U.S.A.

Library of Congress Cataloging-in-Publication Data

Gould, William, 1947–
    VGM business portraits. Apple/William Gould.
        p.   cm.
    Includes index.
    Summary: Introduces basic business concepts, principles, and practices by
focusing on Apple Computer, Inc., its background, growth, and success.
    ISBN 0-8442-4781-2 (alk. paper)
    1. Apple Computer, Inc. —Juvenile literatuire. 2. Computer
industry—United States—Juvenile literature. [1. Apple Computer,
Inc. 2. Computer industry. 3. Computers.] I. Title.
HD9696.C64A8644   1997
338.7′61004165—dc21   97–1796
                                                          CIP
                                                           AC

Manufactured in Belgium by Proost
International Book Production.

Courtesy of Apple Computer, Inc.

BUSINESS PORTRAITS

APPLE

WILLIAM GOULD

VGM Career Horizons
a division of *NTC Publishing Group*
Lincolnwood, Illinois USA

ACKNOWLEDGMENTS

Our thanks to Apple Computer, Inc.
for providing us with copies of their
annual reports and historical publications
from which we drew information to
develop a profile of the company.
Editorial comments made and conclusions
reached by the author about general
business practices of international
companies do not necessarily reflect the
policies and practices of Apple Computer, Inc.

Our thanks also to illustrators Malcolm Porter
and Neil Reed; to photographers John Greenleigh,
Jeff Haeger, Will Mosgrove, Peter Stember/
Apple Computer, Inc; Gill Allen/Times
Newspapers Ltd; and the following companies
who kindly supplied photographs: IBM; Intel;
Xerox Palo Alto Research Center; Adobe Systems;
Time Magazine; Motorola; and Microsoft.

CONTENTS

| People |
| Things |
| Money |

▲ Businesses need people (human resources), things (physical resources) and money (capital).

The adventure of business

Business often sounds difficult but its basic principles are simple, and it can be very exciting. The people involved in the creation and running of the businesses we examine in VGM's BUSINESS PORTRAITS faced challenges and took risks that make some adventure stories seem dull.

What is a business?

If you sell your old computer to your friend for money you are making a business deal. Anyone who produces goods or services in return for money, or who works for an organization that does so, is involved in business.

Businesses try to make profits. They try to sell things for more than the amount the things cost them to make. They usually invest part of the profit they make to produce and sell more of their product. If they have no money to invest, they may borrow it.

The language of business

Many of the technical terms that make the language of business sound complicated are explained on pages 46 and 47.

Business matters

Yellow panels throughout the book explain general business concepts. Blue panels tell you more about Apple.

▼ A business uses money to buy human and physical resources, and from them creates a product or service which it sells for a profit.

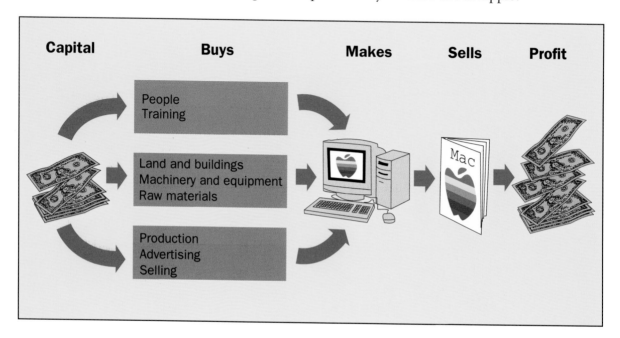

| Capital | Buys | Makes | Sells | Profit |

People
Training

Land and buildings
Machinery and equipment
Raw materials

Production
Advertising
Selling

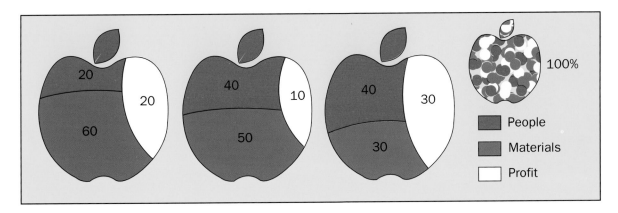

100%

■ People
■ Materials
□ Profit

Apple's business

Apple has been manufacturing computers since 1976. In fact it was the first company ever to make a serious personal computer (PC). It was called the Apple II and helped to start the computer revolution. It could be used for games, but its use as a business tool made it even more popular and helped Apple to grow very fast.

In 1984, Apple introduced its most famous product, the Macintosh. With its bright, graphic screen display, complete with windows, icons, menus and mouse pointer, it completely changed the way people could work with computers. The Macintosh is at the heart of a business that also includes the manufacture of peripherals (printers, scanners, and communications devices), network file servers, operating system software, and applications (word processing applications and database programs). It is at the forefront of the telecommunications and multimedia revolutions, including a series of on-line information services.

▲ Profit is the amount of money earned from sales that is left after all the costs are paid. If an apple sells for one dollar and costs 80 cents to produce and sell, the profit is 20 cents.

Courtesy of Apple Computer, Inc.

▲ The Apple logo is a symbol of quality. It was designed by Rob Janoff in 1977.

◄ The Power Macintosh 9500 is one of a range of fast user-friendly computers that are particularly popular in schools and in the publishing industry.

Courtesy of Apple Computer, Inc.

7

Computers with personality

Whenever you turn on an Apple Macintosh computer, a small drawing of a smiling face appears in the center of a brightly lit screen. Macintosh is happy and ready to go. Moments later, the Mac OS desktop appears, with a list of menu options along the top and icons representing disk drives down the right-hand side of the screen.

▲ The symbol of the Mac Operating System brings a smile to the face of Apple fans.

▶ Children with an Apple computer at home can use skills learned at school for homework, entertainment and Internet research.

APPLE FACTS

* Apple's 1996 revenue was $10 billion.
* It does business in 140 countries.
* It employs 13,000 people.
* There are more than 26 million Macs in operation around the world.
* One in 12 home computers is an Apple Macintosh.
* Apple is the third largest seller of personal computers to business and government organizations in the world. Business and government sales account for 45 percent of its total revenues.
* It holds the number one market share position in education. Sales to students and education institutions account for one-fifth of its total sales.

The Macintosh desktop

Move your mouse pointer to a menu option, click and hold, and down comes a list of actions you can take. Move your pointer over a disk icon, double-click the mouse button, and magically a window opens and more icons appear, like drawings on a piece of paper. Double-click on one of them and, more Mac magic opens another window into a program or document.

Macintosh windows are like sheets of paper. They can overlap, sit on top of each other and be shuffled around like real sheets of paper on a desk. You can type text on them and, thanks to a process called bit-mapping, put your words in different typefaces and add in pictures and panels. Suddenly with your Mac you are equipped with the tools (though not the talents or skills) of a professional printer, artist or designer. You can produce reports, business plans, magazines, brochures, and even whole books, like this one.

The significance of Apple

The Apple Mac and successors such as the PowerBook and PowerMac are computers that work for ordinary people. What makes them so user-friendly is their graphic user interface (GUI, pronounced "gooey"). Before Apple came along, a GUI was nowhere to be seen outside the laboratories of a small group of California computer scientists. Apple brought GUIs into the commercial world and introduced affordable, creative computing to its customers.

Today, from its headquarters in Cupertino, California, Apple runs a global organization employing about 13,000 people. It has manufacturing plants throughout the United States, in Europe, and the Asia-Pacific region. As well as making computers and computer peripherals and producing the software to make them useful, Apple also runs some of the finest computer-training courses in the world.

Courtesy of Apple Computer, Inc.

▲ A page from the World Wide Web created using Apple technology.

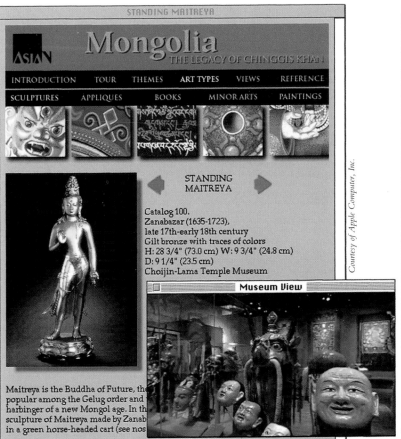

Courtesy of Apple Computer, Inc.

STANDING MAITREYA

Catalog 100,
Zanabazar (1635-1723),
late 17th-early 18th century
Gilt bronze with traces of colors
H: 28 3/4" (73.0 cm) W: 9 3/4" (24.8 cm)
D: 9 1/4" (23.5 cm)
Choijin-Lama Temple Museum

Maitreya is the Buddha of Future, th[e] popular among the Gelug order and [the] harbinger of a new Mongol age. In th[e] sculpture of Maitreya made by Zanab[azar] in a green horse-headed cart (see nos[...])

Maitreya holds the elixir of immortality in his left hand, and his right hand is raised in the gesture of argument. A pleasing contrast of matte and polished surfaces is especially well displayed on this work, with its streamlined limbs and simplified decoration. Maitreya's harmonious, well-balanced form is complemented by a benevolent expression and an elegant radiance.

BUSINESS MATTERS: INNOVATION

Innovation is the act of doing or making something new. People always want the latest thing. If you can invent a new, useful product and make it for a price people can afford, you have the basis of a business success. This is what Apple did. In the 1970s computers were enormous, complicated machines that filled whole rooms. Apple's innovations helped produce powerful computers that you can hold in the palm of your hand.

◀ Why go to the museum when Apple can bring it to your desk? QuickTime VR (Virtual Reality) allows you to view exhibits in the round with this interactive program created for San Francisco's Asian Art Museum.

▲ A tiny Intel Pentium Processor nestles in a flower. The invention of the microchip allowed the development of PCs.

▶ The first fully electronic computer was called ENIAC (Electronic Numerical Integrator And Computer). It had 18,000 valves and filled a room.

THE FIRST COMPUTERS

As long ago as the 17th century, the French mathematician and philosopher Blaise Pascal invented a mechanical calculator with geared wheels. It could add and subtract. In the 19th century, the English inventor Charles Babbage dreamed up a complicated machine called the analytical engine. It could store a set of instructions for solving mathematical equations fed to it on punched cards. Babbage never saw his machine built because he thought (wrongly, as modern science has shown) that 19th-century engineers lacked the necessary precision.

Before Apple

In the 20th century, computers have been through a swifter development than any other form of technology, first using valves, or vacuum tubes, then transistors, and finally microchips. These are tiny wafers of silicon carrying thousands of microscopic electronic circuits. The microchip, or micro-processor, has allowed computer manufacturers to produce smaller and smaller machines, so that today a 9-pound desktop computer costing a thousand dollars has 32 times the speed and memory of a computer that cost millions of dollars to build and filled an air-conditioned room back in the 1940s.

Personal computers

The development of the microprocessor in 1971, by a company called Intel, paved the way for the personal computer. An article in the magazine *Radio-Electronics* in 1974 speculated on how such a computer could be produced. The first use of the new chips came that same year in electronic calculators. Hewlett-Packard, destined to become a major manufacturer of computers and peripherals, introduced a programmable pocket calculator.

Two years later, one of Hewlett-Packard's employees, a technician and frustrated computer designer named Stephen Wozniak, began building his own computer in a garage in Cupertino, California. He and a friend, Steven Jobs, were about to launch a new company and change the world. They were the founders of Apple.

A TALE OF TWO STEVES

Steve Wozniak was born in 1949 and brought up in Cupertino, California. At school he tinkered with electronic devices and once used a piece of equipment called a blue box to fool the machinery at his local telephone company into letting him make free international phone calls. Wozniak dropped out of college and never qualified as an engineer. Hewlett-Packard gave him a job as a lowly technician. Steve Jobs persuaded him to leave and help him to found Apple. Through Apple, Wozniak became a multimillionaire who loved promoting rock concerts. He took little part in the development of the Macintosh and left Apple in 1985. But today he is advising Apple once again.

Steve Jobs was born in 1955 and was a school friend of Steve Wozniak in Cupertino. He studied briefly at Reed College, in Oregon, before joining a company called Atari. Like Wozniak he was a computer enthusiast, but Jobs wanted to make a business out of his hobby. After persuading Wozniak to leave Hewlett-Packard, Jobs provided the early business drive of Apple. He found the financial capital to put it on its feet, and he was the major force behind the development of the Macintosh. A colorful personality, Jobs was very demanding and thoroughly engaged in the project. After serving as Apple's president for four years, he eventually left the company in 1985 and founded another computer firm, called NeXT Inc. In 1997, this company was bought by Apple, and Steve Jobs was back at Apple again.

▼ In a suburban garage, the two Steves began a revolution in computing that continues today.

The birth of Apple

In 1976, Palo Alto was an exciting place to be, if you were a computer enthusiast. Stanford University, Palo Alto's internationally renowned education and research center, was the meeting place of a group of hobbyists called the Computer Homebrew Club. Steve Wozniak was a leading member of this club. Not far away, there was something potentially even more exciting: the Xerox Palo Alto Research Center (PARC). The Xerox Company, famous for its photocopiers, set up PARC in 1971 as a think tank. It attracted the best computer brains from all over the country, people who were

Courtesy of Apple Computer, Inc.

▲ The Apple I was simply a circuit board. Customers had to add a case (like this one), a keyboard and a monitor.

▶ In just 10 years, the Apple I, displayed here by Wozniak and Jobs, became a much-honored museum piece.

Courtesy of Apple Computer, Inc.

determined to find ways to make computers easier and more friendly to use. PARC played a vital role in Apple's development.

Apple I

In March 1976, Steve Wozniak and Steve Jobs finished assembling a computer circuit board in a garage belonging to Jobs' parents. The board had no case, screen or keyboard. It was intended for technically-minded computer hobbyists who wanted to assemble their own machines.

Jobs convinced Wozniak that other enthusiasts would be eager to buy similar circuit boards. So Wozniak abandoned his frustrating job with Hewlett-Packard and helped set up a company to produce and sell the circuit boards. On April 1,

---

BUSINESS MATTERS: ENTREPRENEURS

An entrepreneur is a business owner or manager who is prepared to take risks in order to exploit new business opportunities. Entrepreneurs often invest in untried or original projects in the hope of making a large profit before anyone else gets a chance. They may not be the creators of the product or service they are seeking to exploit, but they recognize its potential. In the case of Apple, Steve Wozniak was the creator of the product, but Steve Jobs was the entrepreneur who saw its potential.

1976, the company was established. Jobs called it Apple, because he once had a vacation job in an orchard. Wozniak's board was its first product, the Apple I.

Getting started

Wozniak showed the Apple I to his friends at the Computer Homebrew Club, and it was an immediate success. But the fledgling company needed money to get the Apple I into production. Jobs sold his Volkswagen van and Wozniak sold his Hewlett-Packard programmable calculator to raise just $1,350. A computer store called the Byte Shop ordered 50 Apple Is, and Jobs used the order to persuade a bank to lend him enough money to buy the parts needed to build the boards at the garage. The first Apple Is went on sale in July. Apple was on its way.

▲ Paul Terell, owner of the Byte Shop, was the first commercial customer to realize the potential of the Apple I. Jobs and Wozniak sold their most treasured possessions to buy the parts they needed to fill the order.

BUSINESS MATTERS: CREDIT AND CAPITAL

You need money to start a business, to buy raw materials and equipment, pay staff, rent or buy an office or factory, pay the costs of advertising and selling your product, and to pay yourself. This money is called capital. People like the two Steves with no money of their own have to borrow money. They can ask the bank for credit, a loan which they will repay with interest, or they can ask individuals or other companies to give them money in exchange for part of the profits of the company. If you borrow from a bank, you have to give it evidence, or surety, that you will be able to repay the money when the time comes. You have to convince investors that they will see a good return on their money. In the 1970s, making personal computers was an untried industry so Apple's backers were taking a financial risk. As it turned out, they made lots of money. People whose business is to invest in new business ventures are called venture capitalists.

Apple grows

In August 1976, Apple was in need of cash to keep itself in business. Steve Jobs went looking for capital. Through Nolan Bushnell, his old boss at Atari, he met Dan Valentine who was a venture capitalist. Valentine put him in contact with the man who would help him shape Apple's fortunes, A.C. (Mike) Markkula.

Markkula knew the computer industry. He had been a marketing manager for Intel, the microchip manufacturer. He believed in the business potential of computers. He was also a millionaire, rich enough to risk a lot of money backing a young company like Apple, which had clearly found a market. By the end of the year the Apple I computer was on sale in ten stores with branches all over the United States.

Courtesy of Apple Computer, Inc.

▲ Mike Markkula came out of retirement to help launch Apple. As well as money, he invested a considerable amount of time, energy and business expertise.

▶ Apple's first premises were soon outgrown as production of the Apple II required more and more employees.

BUSINESS MATTERS: COMPANIES AND CORPORATIONS

A company or corporation is an organization that is legally protected by limited liability. Once it is incorporated its owners and investors risk only the amount of money they have invested. If the company fails and gets into debt, the investors lose only the money they have risked, not all the money they own. Limited companies have to publish their accounts and have them checked by independent accountants called auditors.

Planning for growth

In November 1976, Markkula wrote Apple's first business plan. It laid out the strategy for the company's first ten years. Its main goal was for sales to grow to $500,000 by 1986. In retrospect, it was a modest forecast. Apple passed that figure in half the time.

Apple was incorporated on January 3, 1977. Markkula put $250,000 into the company and formally joined it as chairman of the board. He brought in a friend, Michael Scott, to be Apple's president and chief executive officer. More money soon flowed in from other investors. The company moved out of the garage and into its first factory on Stevens Creek Boulevard, in Cupertino. A year later it moved to its then Cupertino headquarters on Bandley Drive. Soon a whole campus of buildings started to grow.

The expanding Apple

The company was growing quickly. By the end of 1978, Apple's sales had leapt tenfold. In December 1979, the number of Apple employees was 250. A year later it was more

---

APPLE II

Steve Wozniak's Apple II computer, and its successors the Apple II+, the Apple IIe and the Apple IIc, were Apple's best-selling products before the Macintosh went on sale. By the time the last Apple II series computer was sold in 1993, about five million had been sold in nearly 17

years. The Apple II was the first computer to come already tested and assembled in an attractive case, equipped with a keyboard and two games. It was aimed at the ordinary consumer, not the computer hobbyist. Customers plugged it into their own television sets or into a

dedicated monitor. It was the first computer with high-resolution color graphics and it had easy-to-follow instructions.

The Apple II was elegant, useful and fun. It was sophisticated enough for business requirements, cheap enough for ordinary people to buy, and exciting for children.

Courtesy of Apple Computer, Inc.

---

than 1,000. In 1978, the company had a distribution network of 300 dealers. By 1980, its products were being sold through 800 retailers in the United States and Canada and another 1,000 outlets overseas.

A major factor in this growth was Apple's second product, the Apple II. Another Steve Wozniak design, the Apple II was introduced in June 1977. It was the first genuine pre-assembled personal computer to sell to a mass market.

Apple goes public

At first Apple was wholly owned by its two founders, Steve Jobs and Steve Wozniak. Since December 1980, it has been a public company owned by stockholders. Stockholders are private individuals, organizations or institutions who invest in a company by buying portions of it. Each portion is called a share, and the company's shares or a block of them are collectively known as stock.

Each share has a financial value, and the shares are bought and sold on the stock exchange, or stockmarket. Share prices can rise or fall depending on whether the company does well or badly. In return for their money, stockholders have a say in how their company is run and can vote at the company's annual general meeting. If the company does well they receive a share of the profits called a dividend.

▲ Steve Jobs realized the value of good design. It was Wozniak who created the Apple II, but Jobs who insisted that it looked as desirable as the best consumer products.

▶ Suddenly Apple had become a big business. Four years after going public, its assembly lines were unable to churn out computers fast enough.

▼ Computer technology enabled the Apple assembly line to be fully automated with robots performing many operations.

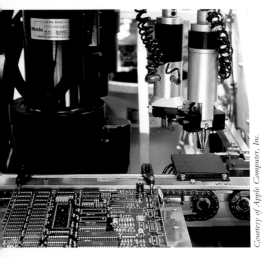

Money for expansion

Companies usually go public when they need extra money to finance expansion. In its first four years from 1976 to 1980, Apple shot to popularity with the Apple II. It also produced the first of a long list of peripherals, add-ons such as interface cards to connect the Apple II to a variety of printers, the Disk II, a floppy disk drive that made serious software like VisiCalc possible, and the Silentype, Apple's first printer.

Apple needed money to extend its network of dealers and to create more new or improved products. It had recently embarked on two revolutionary but expensive projects, the development of the Lisa and Macintosh computers.

A taste for Apples

In December 1980, the first batch of 4.6 million Apple shares went on sale at $22 per share. All the stock was snapped up within minutes. Apple's spectacular early growth made a great impression on potential investors and they were eager to buy into the company. More shares were sold in May 1981.

BUSINESS MATTERS: SPREADSHEETS

The Apple II was the first computer to make an impact on the world of business. VisiCalc, the first electronic spreadsheet, one of the most influential programs in business computing history, was written specially for it. Accountants use spreadsheet programs in place of the many account books that bookkeepers formerly had to write by hand. The computer does all the necessary mathematical calculations and the figures can be printed out in minutes.

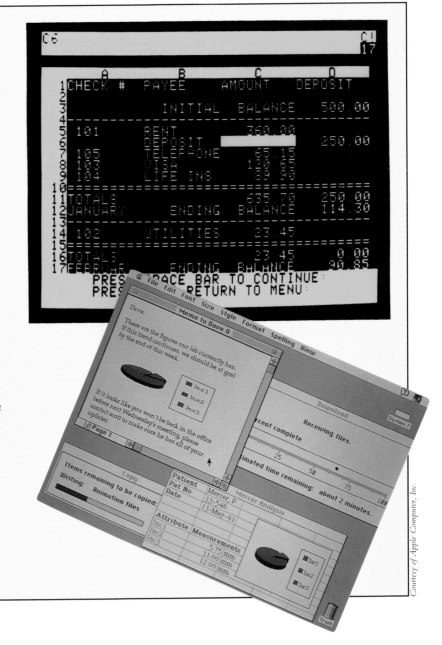

▶ VisiCalc, the first electronic spreadsheet (top), was the forerunner of many modern software programs that allow users the luxury of making continuously changing calculations, and displaying figures in a variety of ways.

A computer called Lisa

The PARC scientists who developed the first practical GUI believed that few outsiders could understand what they were doing and had no idea of its commercial potential. The Xerox Company seemed to regard the project as a sideline and apparently had no plans to develop it commercially.

A trip to the PARC

In December 1979, Apple approached Xerox for some money to fund their new projects. They had just begun work on a new computer called Lisa (after the daughter of one of Apple's engineers). Jobs and his colleagues visited PARC and were shown the Alto, a prototype machine running a GUI.

▲ Scientists at the Xerox PARC facility, building on the work of pioneering engineers Douglas C. Engelbart and Ivan Sutherland, produced a machine that was ahead of its time.

▶ The Alto's simple short-cut devices were a startling innovation.

Many now familiar features were already working on the Alto, including windows, icons, pop-up menus and a mouse. Communicating with computers, even good ones like the Apple II, had always been a laborious time-consuming process. The user sat at a black screen with off-white type on it. To do anything—copy a file or run a program—you had to type in commands. With a GUI, commands were mostly replaced by menu choices that were easy to remember and could be accomplished with the click of a mouse.

The Lisa team was dumbfounded. They left PARC with no money but were fired with enthusiasm for a completely new direction in personal computing. If Xerox was not interested, they would develop it themselves.

BUSINESS MATTERS: PRODUCT AND PRICE

Some companies are profitable because they sell extremely expensive products to a few people who can afford them. But the world's really successful companies are mostly those that sell their products to ordinary people—the mass market. Lisa was a breakthrough in the world of computing, but its price was too high for ordinary people to buy.

Courtesy of Apple Computer, Inc.

◀ The Lisa and the upgraded Lisa 2 (top) were innovative machines, with (below) on-screen graphics, pop-up menus, windows, mouse, calculator and clock.

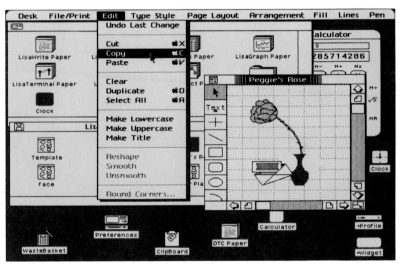

Development of Lisa

Over the next three years the Lisa team worked on the new computer. They had to write complex operating software that brought to life something resembling the PARC system without using PARC's programming code. They made many mistakes, but the Lisa team persisted and completed the project.

An expensive lady

Lisa's programming and the costly new fast microprocessor and other hardware it needed to run the GUI made it an expensive project. Apple spent $50 million developing the Lisa computer. When it went on sale it cost $9,995, a price only large corporations could afford.

BUSINESS MATTERS: RESEARCH

Businesses conduct research to make sure they make the right decisions and keep ahead of their rivals. Scientific research and development (R&D) is carried on within the company to ensure that products are safe and continue to meet high standards of quality and also to see how the products can be improved. Product research or market research are usually carried out by specialist organizations. They ask people to fill out questionnaires or interview them about their likes and dislikes. In the early 1980s, Apple invested a great deal of time and money in R&D but paid little attention to market research. The Lisa (and later the Macintosh) turned out the way they did largely because their designers liked them that way and thought other people would too. They never tested the market to find out. In the 1990s Apple pays much more attention to market testing.

Macintosh the great

The early 1980s were a busy time for Apple, not solely because of the Lisa. The company expanded overseas, opening plants in Ireland and Singapore, and it introduced programming languages—Fortran and Pascal—and interface cards (linking devices) for the Apple II. It introduced its first mass-storage hard disk in 1981 and its first dot-matrix printer in 1982. It also launched the Apple III.

The birth of the Macintosh

Meanwhile, away from the mainstream of Apple's activities, an Apple employee named Jef Raskin dreamed up a computer called the Apple Macintosh. It would have some elements of a GUI, but no mouse. It would not be powerful but it would be portable, affordable and simple to use. It would be efficient and elegant.

Raskin had a prototype of his Macintosh ready by the end of 1979. But there his concept ended. When Steve Jobs was forced off the Lisa project, he discovered the Macintosh, took it over and changed it. Raskin left the company.

Courtesy of Apple Computer, Inc.

▲ The Macintosh was cheap enough to sit on the desks of bosses, secretaries, students and children. It was swift, stylish and simple to use.

Courtesy of Apple Computer, Inc.

▲ Initial sales of the Macintosh encouraged Jobs and Apple's then president John Sculley to overestimate future demand. Sales slumped and the company was left with unsaleable stock.

SHORT ON SOFTWARE?

At first Mac users could use only software produced by Apple itself. The computer was excellent and easy to use but no other applications could run on its system. People were reluctant to spend money on a machine with such a drawback. Many companies have since written exciting software for the Mac. Mac's copious software library today includes word processors from Claris and Microsoft and desktop publishing programs such as Adobe PageMaker, Quark XPress and Adobe Illustrator. With

such programs Apple has become a favorite in the publishing and graphic design industries.

Lisa's little brother

Jobs brought his Lisa experience to bear on the Mac. He ordered a new prototype with a mouse. Development of the Mac in its new form took three years, from 1981 to 1984. Its designers used the same Motorola microprocessor as the one used in the Lisa, but with much less memory. Yet the way in which they put the Mac together made it run twice as fast as the notoriously slow Lisa. Jobs thought his computer "insanely great."

The triumph of the Macintosh

The Mac was launched in January 1984. Its sale price was $2,495—less than a quarter of the price of a Lisa. But although it was faster than the Lisa, it was still slow and underpowered. It did not have enough memory nor a hard drive. After an initial burst of interest, Mac sales dipped. Two factors limiting sales were the unfamiliarity of the GUI and the lack of applications (word processing and other programs) for the Mac. Both these hardware and software limitations have since been overcome.

Meanwhile the Lisa languished. In the spring of 1985 it was renamed the Macintosh XL, but its sales failed to improve and a few months later it disappeared from the Apple catalog forever.

BUSINESS MATTERS: CUSTOMER CONFIDENCE

Before you launch a new product it is essential to get it right. Every detail must be checked. Faulty products are news that travels fast. Recalling and replacing costly items can cripple a company and the nuisance it causes customers stays in their minds. The Apple III was a technological advance over the Apple II. It was a good computer, but a fault in the first batch made customers lose confidence in it. It never sold well and was dropped from the product line in 1984.

◀ Apple's software was perfect for desktop publishing, but owners were often frustrated at not being able to run work created on other systems.

▼ Adobe Photoshop is the world's leading photo design and production software. It allows users to transform photographs as if by magic.

▶ Apple has learned its lesson. Nowadays you could hardly carry all the software programs it will run.

Adobe Photoshop 3.0

Selling Apple computers

In 1977, Apple began shipping its computers to Europe through an independent distributor called Eurapple. By the end of 1980, Apple had the biggest world distribution network in the industry, consisting of 1,800 retailers. Apple's sales team keeps in regular touch with the company's independent dealers. Regular meetings of the Apple Dealers' Councils provide important product feedback to the company.

Shows and specialists

From the start, Apple sold its products through specialist dealers. An important element in Apple's selling strategy was the trade show or exhibition. In 1977, Apple took the largest booth at the first West Coast Computer Fair. Apple's then chairman, Mike Markkula, went around the exhibition signing up dealers to handle the newly unveiled Apple II. Over the years these shows proved so useful that Apple began its own in 1981 with the first Apple Expo. Other shows followed, including separate shows for the Mac and its accessories.

In 1992, Apple began selling through non-specialist superstores for the first time and by direct mail through its catalog. This was largely a response to competition from rival computer firms and poor economic conditions, but it also tied

▲ Distribution is a vital part of marketing. It is no use selling your product if you cannot get it to stores and customers on time.

► Apple Centers offered customers not just a chance to purchase a computer but also free advice from knowledgeable staff who helped with initial training, customer service and the provision of parts and upgrades.

Courtesy of Apple Computer, Inc.

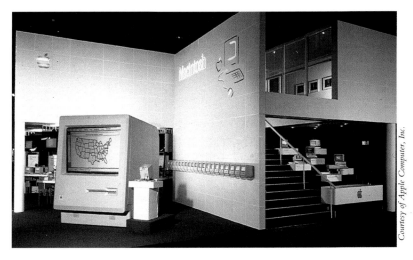

◀ Apple displays its wares at computer exhibitions. Customers are encouraged to try out the mouse and succumb to the computer's charm.

in with the company's aim to provide affordable computing power for everybody, not just computer hobbyists. The strategy did not work. Sales failed to recover.

Price wars

In 1993, Michael Spindler became Apple's chief executive officer (CEO). Over the next two years he tried to reverse the decline in sales by cutting prices. The company produced a host of new cheaper machines but they did not sell well. In 1995, the company lost $69 million. In 1996, Dr. Gilbert F. Amelio was appointed as the new chairman and CEO. Mike Markkula continued to serve as Apple's vice-chairman.

APPLE AROUND THE WORLD

Cupertino is the center of a manufacturing and distribution organization that since 1977 has spread to 140 countries. Major plants in the United States have included Fountain, Colorado; Sacramento, California; and Carrollton, Texas. Apple headquarters in Europe are in Paris, and there is a major plant in Ireland. It has a large plant in Singapore and operations in Africa and the Middle East. Since the early 1990s, Apple's sales have extended into Asia, the Middle East, Eastern Europe and China.

BUSINESS MATTERS: DESIGN FOR SALES

Design is an important part of marketing. Consciously or unconsciously we all make choices about design. If we have a choice between two equally useful products at the same price, most people buy the one that looks more beautiful. Apple computers are designed to make buyers want to take a closer look at demonstration models in shops and exhibitions, and perhaps play with the mouse. Once they get their hands on the machine, they are half way to buying it.

◀ The Macintosh II was nick-named the Little Big Mac. Its sleek, clean design appealed particularly to designers who admired it even as a piece of furniture.

In 1981, when its biggest rival, International Business Machines (IBM), introduced its first PC, Apple took space in *The Wall Street Journal*, America's top financial newspaper, to run an amusing message beginning "Welcome, IBM. Seriously." It was funny at the time, but with IBM-compatible computers now claiming 80 percent of the personal computer market, the smile has faded from Apple's face.

▶ For the 1985 SuperBowl, Apple provided a cushion for every seat in the Stanford Stadium. John Sculley was happy that ticket holders and television viewers alike would remember Apple whichever team won the game.

Advertising Apple

Steve Jobs, himself a colorful personality, realized the value of advertising right from the start. One of the first things he did in 1976 was recruit top Californian advertising agency and public relations firm Regis McKenna to handle Apple's advertising. Regis McKenna's first campaign in 1977 for the Apple II was aimed at computer hobbyists, but it wasn't long before Apple was advertising in consumer magazines, the first computer firm to do so. From 1981 Apple embarked on television advertising. It also bought huge amounts of space in the national press and specialist magazines.

Ads with impact

Apple's advertising agents have came up with some legendary advertisements. The television commercial launching the Apple Macintosh in 1984 hit the headlines. It promised freedom and choice to a nation supposedly deprived of information technology. In November that year Apple bought all the advertising pages in *Newsweek* for a special Mac campaign. In 1985, the company made sure that a huge television audience saw its logo. It paid to have cushions with the symbol placed on every seat of the Stanford Stadium where the SuperBowl was being played.

Courtesy of Apple Computer, Inc.

THE REAL 1984

In his novel *1984*, George Orwell describes life in a society of the future where people have no freedom and no information. The people are oppressed and the state watches over them like "big brother." The time, then in the future, is 1984. When the year 1984 actually

On January 24th,
Apple Computer will introduce
Macintosh.
And you'll see why 1984
won't be like "1984."

arrived, it did not bring with it Orwell's dreadful world. Instead it brought the

Macintosh. The machine's launch was advertised on television on January 22, 1984 in the middle of the SuperBowl. In the ad, an athletic young woman symbolically freed an oppressed people from the nightmare of an information monopoly. The ad was backed up by the message: "Macintosh. Why 1984 won't be like '1984'." The commercial was aired only once, but news bulletins rebroadcast it several times,

and the memory remains.

Targeting the upwardly mobile

Today Apple's global advertising is handled by a company called BBDO. The agency has the job of bringing Apple's name to as wide a public as possible, so Apple advertisements increasingly appear outside specialist computer magazines. Computers are conventional consumer products and are advertised like any other. In the 1990s, Apple has run direct-response campaigns on MTV (Music Television) in an effort to reach college students. It also runs mass newspaper, magazine and radio advertisements for its PowerBook computers.

Recently Apple has run a new series of advertisements that show Macintosh computers alongside BMW cars, famed for their quality. The company is trying to attract people who are prepared to pay a bit extra for something special, something like the Macintosh computers, with a touch of class.

Apple's image

The way that a company appears to the outside world is called its image. Corporations such as Apple have their own public relations departments and hire specialist firms to talk to the public and the media about the company and its products, and present them in the best possible light. They seek to place "good news" stories in the media and try to get good product reviews in computer journals such as *Byte* and in brand-dedicated magazines such as *MacUser*. These people set up meetings and product demonstrations with journalists and broadcasters. What the journalists write is up to them, but it all provides publicity for the company. Apple's best piece of publicity came in late 1982, when *Time* magazine named a personal computer as its "Man of the Year."

Company publicity

Apple's public relations people provide advice and information not only to the press but also direct to the public, especially to special-interest groups such as users' groups and educational organizations. They supply printed literature and audiovisual presentations about Apple and its activities. Since the early 1990s, Apple has also been able to provide information and product support via the Internet.

▲ Normally Time magazine named a man of the year. In 1982, it named the personal computer, acknowledging the importance of the revolution brought about by Apple.

▼ Apple's apple is an object of desire. Used on practical merchandise like these T-shirts and mugs, it enhances the company's youthful, fun image.

SIGN OF QUALITY

Apple Unbreakable Mug $6.00

Apple users love their computers. For them the rainbow-striped Apple trademark symbolizes knowledge, desire and hope. The apple is the fruit of the tree of knowledge, the bite taken from its luscious flesh is a symbol of desire and the rainbow a symbol of hope. The Apple logo is instantly recognizable. It is the company's stamp of quality. It appears on paper in Mac's advertising and promotional material and sits in the top left corner of the Mac screen. Click on it with your mouse and it lets you choose from a host of helpful utilities, including a clock and a calculator. Whatever application you are running, the reassuring Apple is always there.

Company design

The rainbow-colored apple with one bite out of it is a familiar sight on billboards, in the press and on television. Apple hopes that it represents quality in people's minds.

Steve Jobs was insistent that all the company's products should be as thoughtfully designed as its trademark. The Mac had to be a distinctive shape, it had to look good and be easy to use. Even the parts not on view had to be elegant and beautiful. The Mac should have a place in the Museum of Modern Art and Design.

Courtesy of Apple Computer, Inc.

▲ This was Apple's original logo. It was designed by Ron Wayne, who was part of the original "garage team." It shows Sir Isaac Newton being inspired by a falling apple. What sort of image do you think it presents?

◀ Apple public relations and technical staff brief the press and other interested parties about new products.

Every year all public companies produce an annual report. This document explains to stockholders how the company is getting on and includes a summary of the company accounts. The profit and loss account details how much the company has earned from sales and investments, what its costs have been and what its assets are worth. The difference between the company's earnings and its costs is its profit or loss.

▶ Company figures, reports and brochures are easy to design and produce on Apple computers such as this Performa 640CD.

Money matters

No business can exist without money. Apple's capital comes from the sale of its stocks and its products. It uses its money to pay its staff and to develop, manufacture, advertise and sell its products. It also pays for factory and office space and equipment. From its profits it must pay dividends to its stockholders and taxes to the governments of all the countries in which it operates. It may also use surplus profits to invest in other companies.

Profit and loss

At the end of each year Apple, like other companies, adds up what it has earned from selling its products and what it has spent in producing them. If earnings are greater than expenses, then the company has made a profit. If the expenses outweigh the earnings, the company has made a loss. Once Apple made high profits, but recently it has made a loss of over $60 million. It has produced more computers than it can

Courtesy of Apple Computer, Inc.

sell and the unsold inventory sits in warehouses, growing older and less valuable. Inventory has a value if it can be sold. If there is no prospect of selling it, it has virtually no value.

Investments

When companies are doing well and have good prospects, they can raise money for new projects by selling more shares to investors or by selling shares they own in other companies. Apple has earned a good deal by investing in companies with related products. These include the graphics software manufacturer Adobe Systems and General Magic, a company set up by a group of former Apple employees to exploit developments in hand-held computer devices and communications technology. In 1989, Apple sold its nearly three and a half million shares in Adobe for $79 million, but it remains a minority stockholder in General Magic.

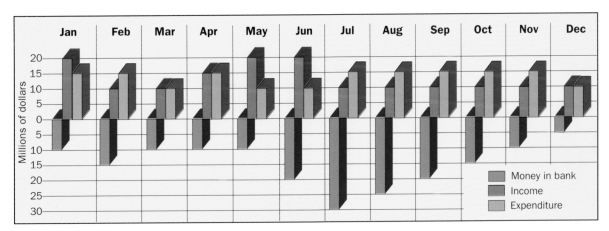

▲ Cash flow can be a problem even for normally profitable companies. If this company had not made so much money in the first half of the year and in the previous year, it would have been in trouble in the second half.

How Apple manages

Apple has a management structure typical of many large businesses. It is organized into divisions. A board of directors controls all of Apple's activities. The board is answerable to Apple's stockholders, who are the owners of the company.

Board of directors

Apple's board of directors makes all the top decisions concerning the company and how it operates. Board meetings are led by the chairman, who controls the agenda (the list of things that the board has to discuss) and makes sure that the meeting runs smoothly. Also on the board are Apple's president (the head of the company) and the chief executive officer (CEO) whose job is to ensure that all the decisions of the board are carried out.

Officials called corporate officers control the work of the divisions and report to the board of directors. They stand at

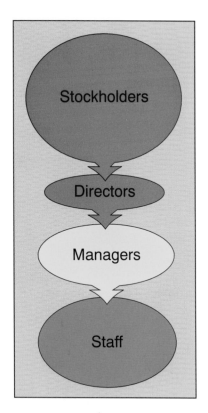

▲ Dr Gilbert F. Amelio was appointed chairman and chief executive officer of Apple in 1996, but left the company in 1997.

▶ The board of directors is answerable to the stockholders. The management and staff are answerable to the board.

the head of a chain of command that passes right down through layers of management to the workers on the assembly line.

Company structure

The company's present organization consists of seven hardware divisions, each responsible for its own financial performance. These are Displays; Newton Message Pad; Performa; Power Macintosh; PowerBook; Printers, Scanners & Digital Cameras; and Servers. In addition there are software, service and Internet divisions and one division devoted to building bridges between Macs and other computers. Claris, a company wholly owned by Apple, produces applications such as word processors and databases. It functions like a company within a company.

▼ Flying the flags at Apple headquarters in Cupertino; running a big business involves coordinating millions of different activities and making them work efficiently together.

▼ A typical board of directors of a large company. In a smaller company one director may have more than one role. In a very small company, there may be only one director.

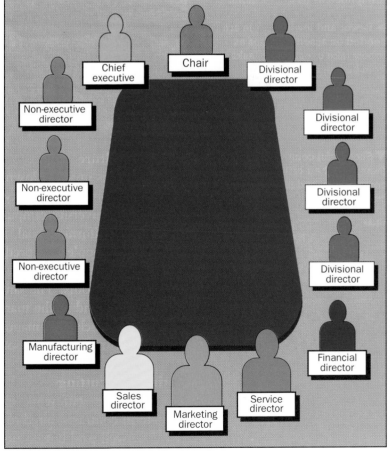

Apple people

Apple's first recruits were a few students who helped the two Steves in their garage-factory. As the company grew rapidly between 1977 and 1980, so did the work force. By December 1980 more than 1,000 people were working for Apple. By 1985, the number was close to 6,000. In 1992, it was closer to 15,000. But with the disappointing sales, the company had to cut back. Nearly 3,000 people lost their jobs in that year. Further staff cuts (1,300 in 1995, 2,800 in 1996) brought the total staff down to 10,000. It is now over 13,000.

Courtesy of Apple Computer, Inc.

▲ Working for Apple is cool! You do not need to be formal to work hard and have good ideas. But Apple is determined to be as disciplined as its competitors.

▶ Fewer and fewer people are needed on assembly lines as robots take over boring tasks from human beings.

▼ Successful companies listen to their staff, their critics, their competitors, and most of all their customers.

Creative culture

Through all its ups and downs Apple has maintained its image as a friendly happy-go-lucky company with an atmosphere more like a university campus than a computer manufacturer. Its style is California casual, and like other companies in the industry its people are predominantly young and talented. They design hardware and software, often enthusiastically working long hours. The same kind of creativity and dedication can be found in the marketing staff and in other areas of the business, including manufacturing, sales, accounts, publicity, administration and personnel.

Caring and cutting

Not all Apple staff work full-time. Almost a third are on short-term contracts, hired to do a job for a fixed period only. They are well paid but do not receive the long-term benefits, such as health insurance and retirement, that full-time employees enjoy. All Apple employees can, however, acquire Apple products on favorable terms (under such programs as the Loan-to-Own plan introduced for the Apple II+ in 1982). They can also receive training at Apple University, an institution launched by Apple in 1983.

In 1988, Apple opened its first childcare center, equipped with Apple Macintoshes not only for administration but also as a learning aid for employees' children. Such measures help to encourage staff loyalty, but with so many job cuts in the past and so many company reorganizations, many Apple workers may feel uncomfortable and insecure.

▲ Cupertino's eating areas have a holiday atmosphere. Staff can sit in the California sunshine, get to know each other, exchange ideas and establish good working relationships.

▲ Time reading magazines is not wasted. It is essential for staff to keep up to date with technology, business, politics and every sphere of life.

▶ Time spent at the piano is not wasted. Apple offers staff and visitors excellent facilities for rest and relaxation, and creative activities.

Apple in the community

Apple believes in helping people to lead healthier, safer lives. This philosophy forms the basis of Apple's charitable giving and its employee volunteer programs. Apple launched its Community Affairs office in 1982. A year later, it founded its Employee Volunteer Action Program. Under this program, Apple employees are encouraged to give up some of their spare time for community projects. In Singapore, for example, employees escort senior citizens on recreational trips, stage events for children in hospitals, and organize campaigns to provide food for refugees.

School and college students have benefited from Apple's generous gifts and price reductions.

Apple volunteers have run many programs to help even the youngest children become computer literate.

Courtesy of Apple Computer, Inc.

BUSINESS MATTERS: CHARITABLE DONATIONS

In many countries, companies gain certain tax advantages by donating money to charitable organizations. These advantages allow them to keep more of their profits than they otherwise could and so encourage them to make further charitable gifts. For the company, charitable donations are a great help in securing goodwill .and publicity. They also benefit the government, since it would have to pick up the welfare bill if certain charities did not exist.

Giving money and equipment

Apple makes donations through its Corporate Grants Department in the form of essential equipment to community-based organizations. These have included agencies supplying services to AIDS victims and local groups seeking economic development for inner-city areas. Apple also leads the way in providing computer technology that helps disabled people to live more independent lives. Its products include such built-in features as on-screen text and image magnification for people with impaired vision.

The environment

Protecting the environment is a main part of Apple's work in the community. In 1992, it eliminated the use of ozone-hostile chlorofluorocarbons (CFCs) from its manufacturing processes. It also launched a program to allow customers to recycle used toner cartridges from Apple laser printers.

Every year Apple donates equipment to environmental groups around the world. The company's EarthGrants program provides academic institutions working on environmental research with computers to help them with data analysis, monitoring of results, education and telecommunications.

Education

In 1979, the Apple Education Foundation was set up to grant Apple systems to schools that would develop classroom software and integrate computers into the curriculum. The following year the company announced AppleSeed, a computer literacy project designed to provide computer materials for both primary and secondary schools. The company offered Apple products to secondary-school and university students at reduced prices and also offered training scholarships to teachers.

▼ Using WorldScript software, Apple provided 30,000 delegates to this Beijing conference with access to the Internet and e-mail in 27 languages.

Courtesy of Apple Computer, Inc.

▲ The PowerPC chip was developed jointly with IBM and Motorola. With standard technology, customers will be able to make freer choices.

Competition

At the end of 1981, there were about 100 companies in the United States manufacturing personal computers. Among them Apple was riding high. The two Steves were multi-millionaires. More than 650,000 Apple computers were in operation throughout the world. Surveys suggested that four out of five Americans had heard of Apple as a computer company. Apple was a household name.

IBM and Microsoft

IBM (International Business Machines), the company that had for years dominated the soon-to-be-defunct main-frame computer market, entered the PC market only in 1981. It licensed its operating system from the Seattle software company Microsoft and used an Intel microprocessor that anyone else could use. Its product could be copied—and it was. Hundreds of independent firms sprang up, manufacturing machines using Intel chips and running the same programs as the IBM ones. Microsoft grew fat from licensing the use of its operating system MS-DOS to the makers of these so-called IBM clones.

A TALE OF TWO SYSTEMS

The Macintosh was not an insanely great seller even though it was in most ways superior to its rivals. It ran on the Mac Operating System and used a Motorola chip. Both were exclusive to Apple. Nobody could copy its machines or license its system. Most other PCs ran on the rival MS-DOS system owned by Microsoft. Instead of creating its own system or buying MS-DOS outright, as it could have done, IBM chose to license the system from Microsoft. It also failed to secure exclusive rights to the Intel processor it used. Both these business mistakes cost IBM dearly and benefited Microsoft. Apple's decision not to license its superior operating system also played into Microsoft's hands.

BUSINESS MATTERS: COMPETITION

Competition for customers forces up standards as firms try to outdo each other in product quality and business efficiency. It also keeps prices down. Without competition businesses can charge what they like. But with competition, rival firms seek to attract customers by charging lower prices than their competitors. But competition has its disadvantages. In some cases it forces companies to reorganize, contract, or go out of business and people lose their jobs as a consequence.

Windows of opportunity

In 1982, while working on the Macintosh, Steve Jobs asked Bill Gates, the owner of Microsoft, to design software for the new computer. This gave Gates, an acknowledged computer and business wizard, access to the workings of the Macintosh Operating System which was more advanced and more user-friendly than his own MS-DOS.

John Sculley, the former boss of PepsiCo, had joined Apple to help promote the Macintosh. He did not see eye to eye with Steve Jobs, and Jobs left the company.

Courtesy of Apple Computer, Inc.

◀ In October 1991, IBM and Apple signed a deal to develop RISC technology together. Apple needed the help of its old enemy in its battle with Microsoft.

Victory for Microsoft

In 1986, Microsoft introduced Windows, built to run on the IBM PC and clones. It quickly became the industry standard. Macintosh was sidelined. Apple still produced superb computers but they were not compatible with other PCs and could not run Windows.

Apple accused Microsoft of illegally copying the Mac system and in 1988 took the giant software corporation to court. After five years' litigation, Apple lost the case. Meanwhile, Windows swept the market.

WHOSE GUI IS IT, ANYWAY?

In December 1989, Xerox Corporation took Apple to court, challenging the validity of its copyrights on the Lisa and Macintosh GUIs. A District Court threw out most of Xerox's arguments. The lawsuit was filed exactly ten years after Apple's visit to the Xerox Palo Alto Research Center. Xerox could perhaps claim that the ideas behind Apple's ground-breaking GUIs were those of its employees and were its property. But in reality the PARC community simply gave form to concepts that went back to the 1960s and earlier. Where Xerox failed to develop what its PARC scientists produced, Apple succeeded, as did Microsoft. As Bill Gates put it: "We both broke into PARC hoping to steal the TV set." They came out with knowledge which only they had the vision to use.

◀ With the power of a great cat, Microsoft's Windows 95 has swept the market that Apple created. Now Apple's future depends on cooperation with Microsoft.

Apple in decline

It was not just competition from rivals that Apple faced in the 1990s, but a decline in the world economy as a whole. Demand for computers was low. From 1990, Apple dropped the price of some of its products and brought out several low-cost items, including some of its laser printers, and the Macintosh Classic, the Macintosh LC and the Macintosh IIsi. A short-lived upturn in sales prompted the company to open a new manufacturing and repair facility at Fountain, Colorado.

Other low-cost products followed in later years as part of a strategy to increase Apple's share of the market in cheaper home computer systems. Notable among them was the Macintosh Performa range and the Macintosh PowerBook (Apple's first notebook computer, introduced in 1991). Some of these products were successful but the range was too great and sales were far lower than expected. The price war was a near disaster.

Microsoft marches on
In 1995, Microsoft introduced Windows 95, an updated

▲ The sheer number of PCs already in use made Windows 95 an immediate and lasting success.

MAC V WINDOWS

Windows 95 is a great advance on its predecessor Windows 3.1. For one thing, you can use meaningful phrases instead of strictly limited character groups as names for your files. For another, Windows 95 gives you enhanced multimedia capabilities and built-in access to a host of on-line information services offered by Microsoft. The trouble is, neither of these benefits is new. Apple introduced sensible filenames along with the Macintosh in 1984. Even the original Mac had a high-performance sound card, and later developments such as QuickTime added an ability to show animations and movies. It launched eWorld, its own set of on-line services, in 1994.

Personal LaserWriter printer

Macintosh II

Macintosh LC

Macintosh Classic, Stylewriter and System 7 software

version of its GUI. Though superior to the old Windows, most of its features had been familiar to Mac users since 1984. Sadly for Apple, it had one big advantage. People already owned about 150 million PCs, on many of which users could install and run Windows 95. News from Apple was so negative in 1995 that then chief executive Michael Spindler took out full-page newspaper advertisements advising customers to: "Rest assured: Apple's mission remains as vibrant today as it was in 1976."

What went wrong?

Today only about one in twelve personal computers is an Apple. The rest are IBM PCs or clones. Why was it that Apple was unable to beat the competition and the recession? Many people think that Apple made two big mistakes. First, it lost its monopoly of the technology and ideas behind its operating system, allowing Microsoft to market virtually the same product. Secondly, it refused to license its operating system to other companies. This meant that instead of becoming the industry standard, its computers remained exclusive and incompatible, and until recently could not run IBM-compatible software.

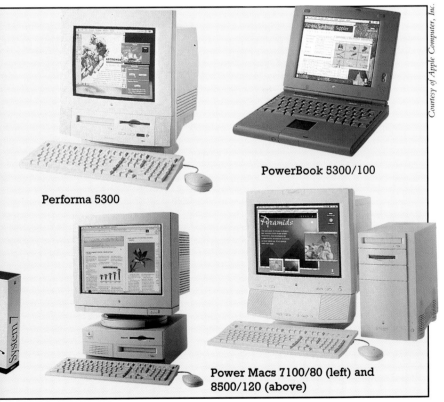

Performa 5300

PowerBook 5300/100

Power Macs 7100/80 (left) and 8500/120 (above)

System

BUSINESS MATTERS: BOOM AND BUST

When economic conditions are unfavorable, a nation's business activity goes into decline, or recession. Fewer goods and services are bought, sold or produced. As a result, unemployment rises. Unemployed people have little money to spend, so even fewer goods and services are produced. During a recession, businesses try to cut their costs, increase productivity, and use every means they can to raise demand. If they cannot, they may collapse completely and go bankrupt.

Times of high prosperity, when people have more money to spend, are called booms. During a boom, businesses flourish because demand for their products is high. If demand grows too high, businesses may try to control it by raising prices. Inflation occurs when prices rise and outstrip wages. Then money falls in value, demand drops and this triggers a recession.

◀ A stream of first- and second-rate products came from Apple in the mid-1990s. Customers were confused. It was simpler to buy a PC.

Fighting back

With 26 million loyal customers and an excellent range of products, Apple has a firm basis for recovery. The company has publicly admitted its mistakes. It has taken many painful steps to cut costs and it has set about reversing its policies.

Friendly Apple

In 1991, Apple and IBM had finalized an agreement to jointly develop a computer technology called RISC (Reduced Instruction Set Computing), which greatly increased computer speed. RISC computers require a special microchip, made in this case by Motorola, a company long associated with Apple.

The first fruit of the cooperation between Apple, IBM and Motorola was the Power Macintosh, introduced in March 1994. Driven by a RISC chip called a PowerPC, it is 12 times

▲ Light enough and small enough to fit in a back-pack, the eMate 300 allows students to work for long periods of time (28 hours) wherever they want. They can operate menus by touching the screen and draw directly onto the screen.

Courtesy of Apple Computer, Inc.

FACE TO FACE

With Apple's QuickTime videoconferencing technology, there is no need to leave your office or classroom to consult your colleagues. A number of people can work on the same project without ever meeting face to face. The QuickTime Media Layer (QTML) brings music, videoanimation, videoconferencing and virtual reality environments to the Internet.

| QuickTime | QuickTime VR | QuickTime Conferencing | Speech | QuickDraw 3D |

Courtesy of Apple Computer, Inc.

as fast as the original Macintosh. Thanks to an agreement between AppleSoft, Apple's software division, and Microsoft, the PowerMac can also run both Macintosh and IBM-compatible software and can share information across the two operating system formats. Mac users are able to run some of Microsoft's successful software products, including Word and Excel, which have been specially adapted for the Mac. This has helped boost the popularity of the PowerMac and its success is already assured with more than a million sales in its first year. The Performa, which uses the same chip, compares well with the Compaq Presario and top-of-the-line IBM clones and can run both Mac and non-Mac software.

Computers on the move

Like the PowerBook, the hand-held Newton Personal Digital Assistant (PDA), introduced in 1993, allows people to carry their computers with them and work on the move, send electronic mail to their colleagues, or link their machines to an office computer whenever they like. In June 1994, Apple launched its first series of on-line subscription services, called eWorld.

▲ Apple's strength is in inventing new products and making them useful, attractive and pleasant to handle.

▼ The Newton Message Pad faces fierce competition from Psion and Hewlett-Packard who are better known in the personal-organizer market.

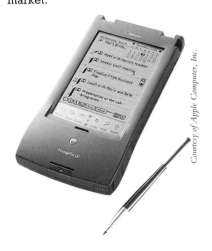

Courtesy of Apple Computer, Inc.

Tomorrow's Apple

Nobody doubts that Apple has the technological know-how to produce the right products for the future. Its future operating system promises to be as innovative as its first. A television-based multi-media Internet browser called Pippin will be a revolution for home customers, and Apple plans to sell it to the two-thirds of people who have no intention of buying a home computer but would perhaps like access to the Internet. Apple will not build the Pippin hardware. It will be manufactured by a Japanese partner.

If you can't beat them . . .
Unable to beat them, Apple is increasingly joining its competitors. From now on Apple will work with, rather than against, the rest of the computer industry. The first Apple clones are on the market and other manufacturers are using its

▲ Up and down go Apple's fortunes. The company's most glorious days may be in the past, but its future will be bright if it maintains its creative vision.

▶ You won't need a computer with Pippin. It will let you browse the Internet through your television.

Courtesy of Apple Computer, Inc.

Prototype

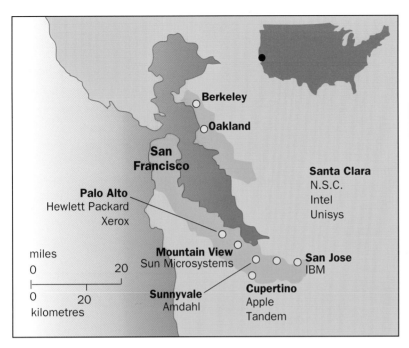

◀ Silicon Valley on the outskirts of San Francisco in California where Apple sits surrounded by friends and enemies.

Map labels:
Berkeley
Oakland
San Francisco
Santa Clara
N.S.C.
Intel
Unisys
Palo Alto
Hewlett Packard
Xerox
miles
0   20
0   20
kilometres
Mountain View
Sun Microsystems
Sunnyvale
Amdahl
Cupertino
Apple
Tandem
San Jose
IBM

PARTNERING

Apple has reached PDA technology licensing agreements with firms such as Sharp, Siemens, Motorola, and Toshiba. It is developing a laptop computer with IBM that will be Macintosh-compatible. It has a budget of $20 million for co-marketing activities with other software developers. It has talked to Microsoft about areas where the two companies can benefit from cooperation. Apple is also cooperating with Oracle, Sun Microsystems and Netscape to set a standard for a network computer NC that will work without a chip and derive its power from other computers via the Internet.

operating systems. Their machines may not have the distinctive look and feel of Apple products but they will allow Apple to sell its software to a bigger market.

Apple will aggressively license its software and to make this easier it will consolidate all the versions of its operating system into one. As well as cutting costs, the company will halve the number of models it produces.

In August 1997, Steve Jobs announced that Microsoft was investing $150 million in Apple, a seven percent share. The two companies also signed patent and technology licensing deals to benefit them both.

Changing image

Instead of going for the cut-price home computer market, Apple will concentrate on the more expensive end of the market, making computers for businesses and institutions. The company wants to add value to its products. It wants them to be like high-performance cars, superbly engineered, good looking, smooth and fast. It will price them just above those of the competition but give them more inherent value. An Apple computer will be a status symbol.

All these measures should be enough to ensure a turn-around for Apple. The company has recovered from previous financial disasters and it has the necessary will and skill to return to profitability and live up to its e-mail address: Apple-Forever@apple.com.

Courtesy of Apple Computer, Inc.

▲ Apple knows who its future customers will be from its Classrooms of Tomorrow project.

Create your own business

▲ Ask your clients to pay in advance for a series of lessons.

Apple makes money by producing and selling computers and the software to run them. But it also sells computer training courses and so do many external organizations. See if you can run a business selling brief training courses on a computer.

Most people over the age of about 30 never learned about computers in school, so you have an advantage over them. With more and more businesses using computers, people like your parents could probably do with a bit of help in learning the basics of computing.

Planning and research
Before you start, think about how you will run your business and get permission from your school and parents before you approach any clients. Find out what the demand is for your service. Who will be your clients and what will they need? They will not all want to be trained for the same type of computer or software. How many customers can your business handle? How much will they be willing to pay for an hour's lesson? How much will it cost you? If you are going into people's homes or inviting people to yours, check that you and your possessions will be safe. You may want to limit your clients to people you know personally.

People
Select a small management team. You will need someone to take care of money, someone to handle the publicity about your courses, people to design and run the courses and people to sell them. Make sure your instructors are capable and reliable, and have good presentation skills.

Capital
You or your clients will probably already have the equipment you need—your home or school computer, peripherals such as a printer and modem, software and documentation. Besides that, you will need capital to produce sales materials,

LABOR

CAPITAL

EQUIPMENT

MARKETING

PROFIT AND LOSS ACCOUNT		
Sales		500.00
Less Cost of Sales		
Equipment	100.00	
Brochures	60.00	
Software	90.00	
	250.00	(250.00)
Gross profit		250.00
Less Overhead		
Rent	20.00	
Stationery	30.00	
Travel	5.00	
Telephone	20.00	
	75.00	(75.00)
Net profit		175.00
Loan repayment	100.00	
Interest	5.00	
	105.00	(105.00)
Net profit after interest		70.00

▲ Proper businesses present their figures as a profit and loss account like this.

course notes and any programs and upgrades you do not already have. If you contribute your allowance money, your parents will be more willing to lend you money. You will have to repay your investors with interest.

Costing

Make a plan for your business. Write down how much you will spend and how much you will charge. Remember your overhead, items like bus fares, stationery and postage. Add up all the costs. Figure out how many computer lessons you must sell to cover your costs and get back all the money you have spent. This is your break-even point. Anything more and you make a profit; anything less and you create a loss. Think of ways to cut costs. Teaching several people together will make more money for the business, so you can afford to cut the cost for joint lessons. Remember to set a fee for telephone consultations.

Selling

To attract interest in your computer lessons, produce an informative brochure that describes exactly what you will offer your clients. Stage a demonstration to show the full range of the training you are able to offer. Place an ad in the school magazine or on the school bulletin board.

Ask fellow students to take your brochure home. Create a story with a good angle for the local paper: "Kids turn teachers," perhaps.

Profit and loss

Keep a record of everything you spend and receive. If you make a large profit, you will have to pay your investors and decide what to do with the rest of the money. Should you split it among yourselves, donate it to a charitable organization or your school (if you were a real company, you would have to pay tax on your profits), or put it back into the business. What would Apple do?

The language of business

Accessory Extra piece of equipment.

Accountant Person who keeps or inspects accounts.

Advertising Making publicly known. Advertisers use television, radio, and newspapers to tell everyone how good their product is.

Agenda A list of items to be discussed at a meeting.

Analysis The process of examining something minutely.

Application A computer program, such as a word processor or spreadsheet, used for a specific task.

Assets Anything owned by a business, including property, money, goods and machines.

Auditor An independent accountant who checks a company's accounts.

Bankruptcy The state of being bankrupt, with no money in the bank and no means of paying debts.

Billion A thousand million or, in Britain, a million million. Billions in this book are a thousand million.

Bit-mapping An electronic process that divides a computer screen into thousands of individual squares called pixels, allowing each pixel to have its own alterable color.

Board of Directors See Directors.

Bookkeeper A person who systematically records a company's business transactions.

Boom A time of prosperity when customers can afford to buy products and business is good.

Brand The name of a company's product. See also Trademark.

Break-even The point at which income from sales equals the cost of production and sales.

Business An organization that sells goods or services.

Capital Money needed to start a business and keep it going.

Cash flow The rate at which money enters and leaves a business during a set period.

Chairman The person who leads a committee or board of directors. Also called a chairperson or chair.

Chief executive The highest-ranking person in a company who has full power to act and make decisions on behalf of the company.

Chip See Microchip.

Chlorofluorocarbons (CFCs) Chemicals that attack the ozone layer in the earth's atmosphere.

Circuit board An insulating board carrying electronic circuits.

Clone An exact copy of an organism or computer.

Commercial 1 Involved in or connected with buying and selling. 2 A radio or TV advertisement.

Company Organization of a group of people who carry on a business. Companies may be small or large, public or private. See also Corporation.

Competition The struggle for customers and profits between two or more enterprises in the same field.

Consumer The final purchaser or user of an article. See also Customer.

Corporate officers Senior directors or managers of a corporation. They include the chief executive officer, the president, the executive officers and vice-presidents. See also Directors.

Corporation Business corporations are usually large, centrally organized public companies.

Costs The amount of money it takes to make or sell a product or service; costings are forecasts of the costs.

Credit To give credit is to allow time for a payment to be made.

Customer Anyone who buys from a seller, especially one who buys regularly.

Customer service Assistance and repairs available to a customer for a set time after buying a product.

Data Information, especially that processed by a computer.

Database A computer program that allows a quantity of information to be stored for easy retrieval.

Dealer A person or company whose business is to buy and sell a specific kind of product, such as cars or computers.

Demand The amount of a product that people are prepared to buy.

Desktop publishing Producing leaflets, pamphlets, books or other documents by means of a computer and printer.

Direct-response campaign An advertising campaign that invites customers to buy direct from the company.

Directors People who guide the activities of a company and make its most important decisions. See also Corporate officers.

Disk A device on which data is stored and from which it can be retrieved by a computer.

Disk drive A computer device that houses and spins a fixed or removable disk, enabling it to be read or written on.

Diskette See Floppy disk.

Distribution The means by which a company's products reach its customers.

Diversification The widening of a range of goods and services.

Dividend A small amount of a company's profits paid to stockholders.

Document A piece of text with or without pictures produced by a word processor or similar application.

Dot-matrix A kind of printer.

Earnings Money earned by a person working, or a company selling.

Employee A person who works for an employer (another person or company) in return for wages or a salary.

Entrepreneur An enterprising person who takes business risks.

Executive director A director who works for a company. A non-executive director is a member of the board but is not employed by the company. See also Directors.

File server A large computer used for storing and retrieving data by other computers linked to it and to each other in a network.

Financial To do with money.

Firm Another word for a business or company.

Floppy disk A removable disk used for storing computer data. See also Disk and Hard disk.

Goods Things other than food produced by a business.

Graphic user interface (GUI) The computer-screen display made of windows, icons, menus and a mouse pointer that makes using a PC easy.

Graphics Computer-created images and pictures.

Hard disk A non-removable computer disk used for the mass storage of computer data.

Hardware Computers and other devices and machines. See also Software.

Health insurance Medical benefits provided by a company.

Human resources The people who work for a business. Also called staff or personnel.

Icon In a graphic user interface, a small picture that stands for a program or document.

Image 1 A picture or piece of art. 2 The way a company appears to the public.

Income Any money that comes into a business in the form of earnings or investments. Also called revenue.

Incorporate To form a legally recognized company.

Inflation A steep increase in all prices.

Innovation The introduction of something new, such as a product, technique or organization.

Interest Money paid to investors for use of the money they have lent.

Interface card A circuit board that plugs into a computer and forms a bridge between it and an external device, such as a printer.

Internet The worldwide network of computers.

Inventory Products stored ready for sale by a company.

Invest To put money into a business or buy shares in it.

Laser printer A kind of printer that uses laser technology.

License Permit that allows someone to make or sell someone else's product.

Logo Short for logogram; a symbol that represents a word and is often used as a trademark.

Loss The money that a business loses when it spends more than it earns. See Profit.

Management The control or organization of a business or a part of it.

Market research Surveying people's tastes and requirements to assess the demand for a product.

Market The total number of buyers and sellers of a product.

Marketing All the activities involved in putting a product on the market, including research and development, distribution and sales, pricing and promotion.

Mass market The majority of the population. Mostly low-priced products sell to the mass market.

Menu A list of actions or tasks from which a computer user can choose.

Merchandise 1 Commercial goods that are bought and sold. 2 To license the use of a logo or character to promote the sales of other products, such as clothes and mugs.

Microchip Tiny piece of silicon that carries on its surface thousands of microscopic electronic integrated circuits. Often simply called a chip.

Microprocessor An electronic circuit on a microchip that performs the basic functions of a computer's central processing unit, or "brain."

Modem A device that connects a computer to a telephone line.

Monitor Visual display unit of a television or computer.

Mouse A hand-held device that moves a pointer on a PC screen, allowing the user to interact with a program.

Multimedia The combination of pictures, sound and text in a computer application, such as a computer game, a CD-ROM encyclopedia, or a Website.

Non-executive director See Executive director.

On-line information service A service that passes information held on a distant file server to a user's computer.

Operating system The software that allows a computer to communicate with its user and run basic programs.

Overheads General costs, such as rent, heating and stationery, that do not relate to a specific operation or item.

Peripheral An external device or machine physically connected to a PC. Peripherals include CD-ROM drives, printers and modems.

Personnel See Human resources.

Physical resources Things such as buildings, machines and raw materials that a business uses.

PowerPC A very fast microprocessor developed for a new generation of computers.

President The head of a country or company.

Price The amount of money for which something can be bought or sold. Price is usually determined by supply and demand.

Product The thing that a business sells. Products can be goods or services.

Profit The difference between what a company earns—its income—and its costs.

Program A list of instructions, written in a programming language, to be carried out by a computer.

Prototype An early trial version of a product.

Public company A business that offers shares of itself for sale to the general public.

Publicity News or information about a company's activities or products.

Raw materials Ingredients for making or manufacturing things.

Recession A time of unfavorable economic conditions when demand for goods is low.

Recycle To reuse materials instead of throwing them away.

Retailer Business such as a store or supermarket that sells goods in small numbers direct to the public. Retailers generally buy their goods from wholesalers who buy in bulk from manufacturers.

Retirement plan A method of saving money to provide a retirement income. Often both employers and employees contribute.

RISC Reduced instruction set computing, a technology for making microprocessors work more rapidly.

Salary Money paid in fixed amounts, usually monthly, to "white-collar" workers.

Shareholder A person who owns shares in a company.

Shares Tiny portions of a company's capital value. The price at which shares are bought and sold goes up and down according to the company's success. See also Stock.

Software Computer programs in general. See also Hardware.

Sound card A device installed in a computer for generating or processing sounds or music.

Spreadsheet A computer application used for keeping running accounts.

Stock A block of shares.

Stock market Exchange where stocks and shares are bought and sold. Also called a stock exchange.

Stockholder Person who holds stock.

Subsidiary A business partly or wholly owned by another.

Surety Security given to a bank, lender or supplier as a guarantee that the debt will be repaid.

Tax Money that businesses and individuals have to pay the government from their earnings.

Technology The application of science to industry.

Think tank A group of experts brought together to make an extensive study of a subject.

Toner The powdered ink used in a photocopier or laser printer.

Trademark A name, design, symbol or some distinguishing mark that makes a company or product unique and recognizable.

Transistor A device used in electronics before the invention of the microchip.

Unemployment Lack of paid work. Levels of unemployment rise during a recession.

Upgrade A new, improved version of a program or piece of hardware.

Valve A device, also called a vacuum tube, used in computers, radios and television sets before the invention of the transistor.

Venture capitalist A wealthy investor (or company) who puts money into a new business enterprise without owning it.

Virtual reality A computer-generated environment that seems almost real to the person who experiences it.

Wage Weekly payment made to manual workers on an hourly rate.

Website An address on the WorldWideWeb where a person or company presents information to other users.

Window A rectangular area on a computer screen in which the icons for various programs appear.

Word processor A computer application used to prepare text.

World Wide Web A vast collection of multimedia information held on computers all over the world and open to any user through the Internet.

Index